to Brendan / walk with me

OOGACHTEND

re/collection
impressions from the road

ephameron

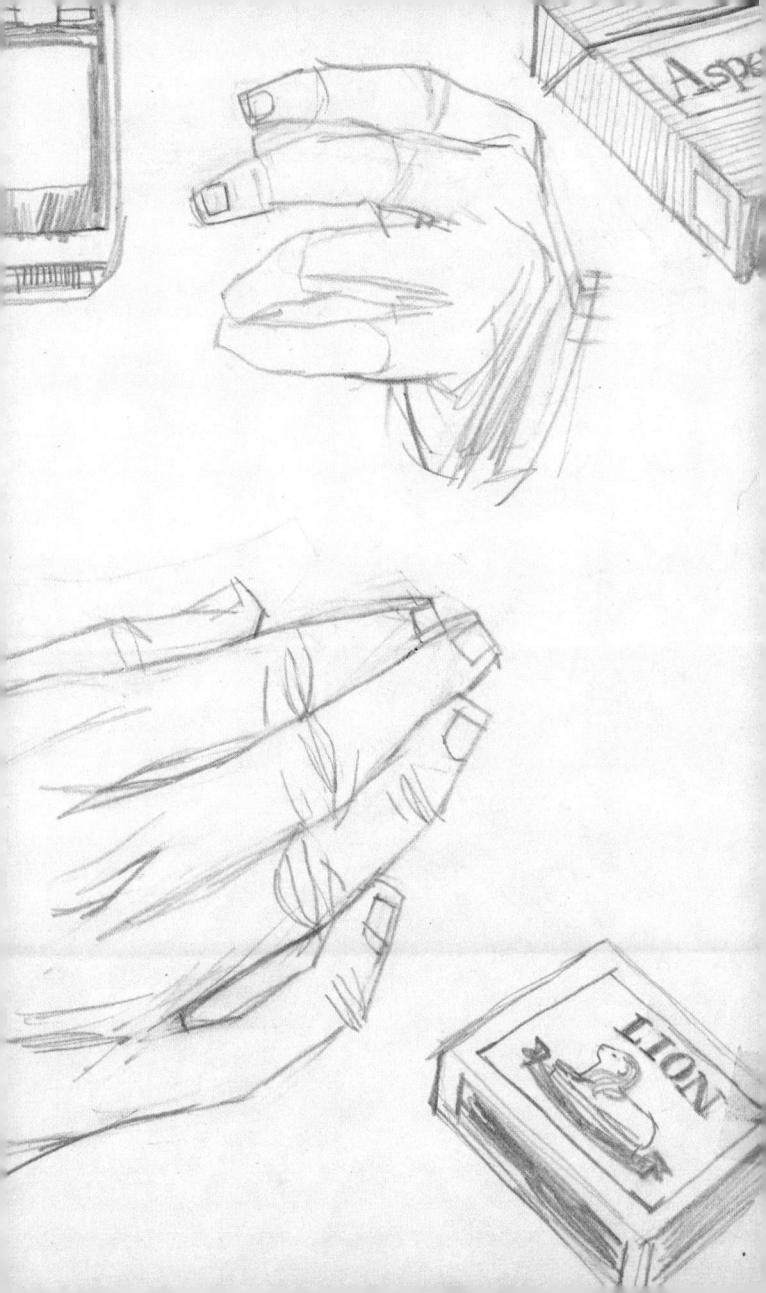

TILL

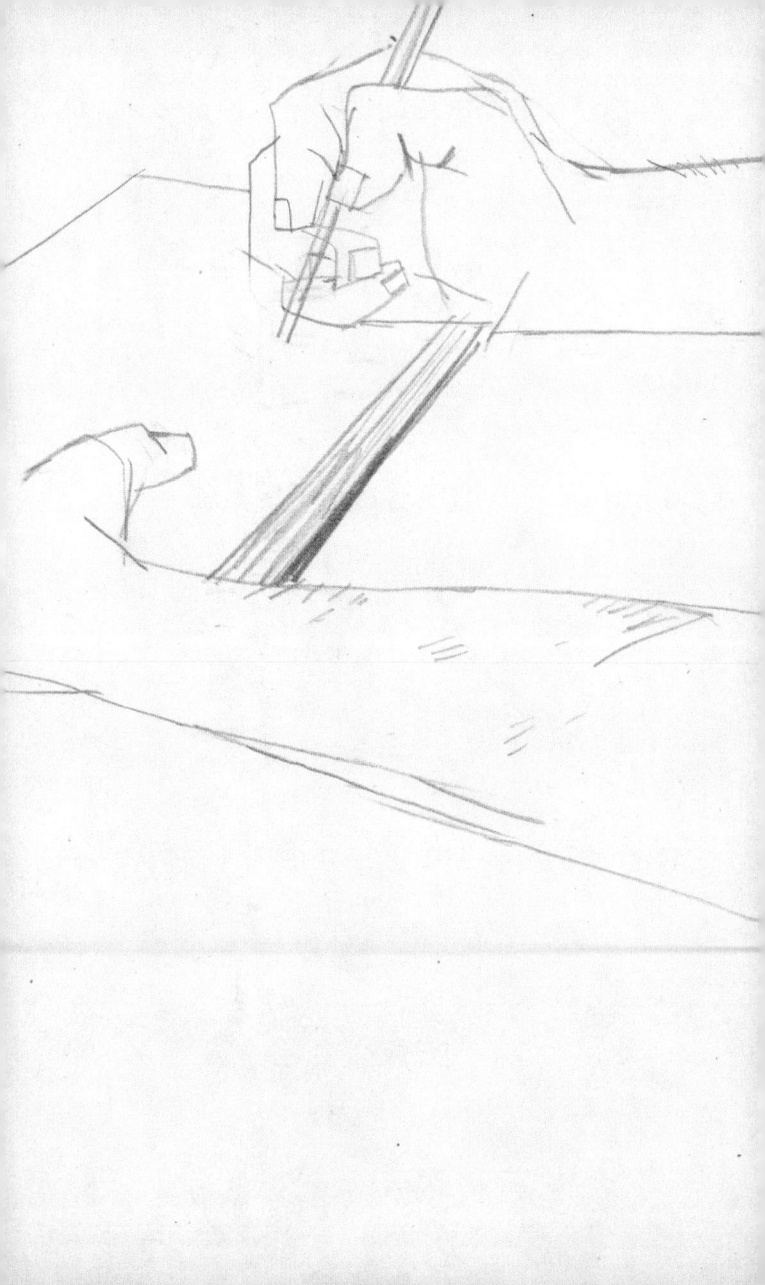

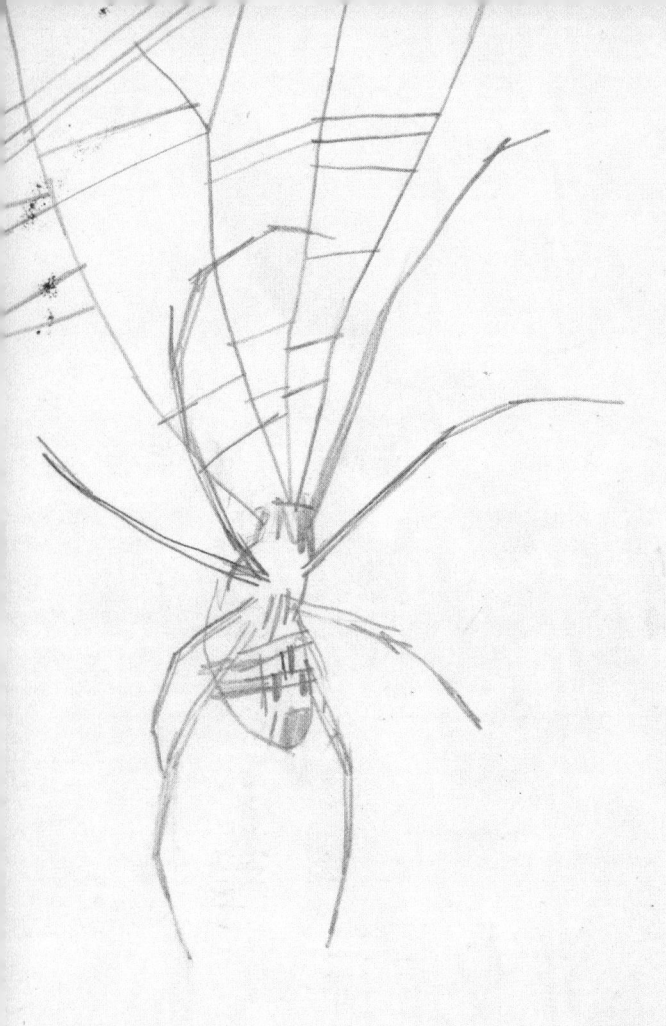

TROUVILLE

SEAPORT VILLAGE
SAN DIEGO

SILVERLAKE

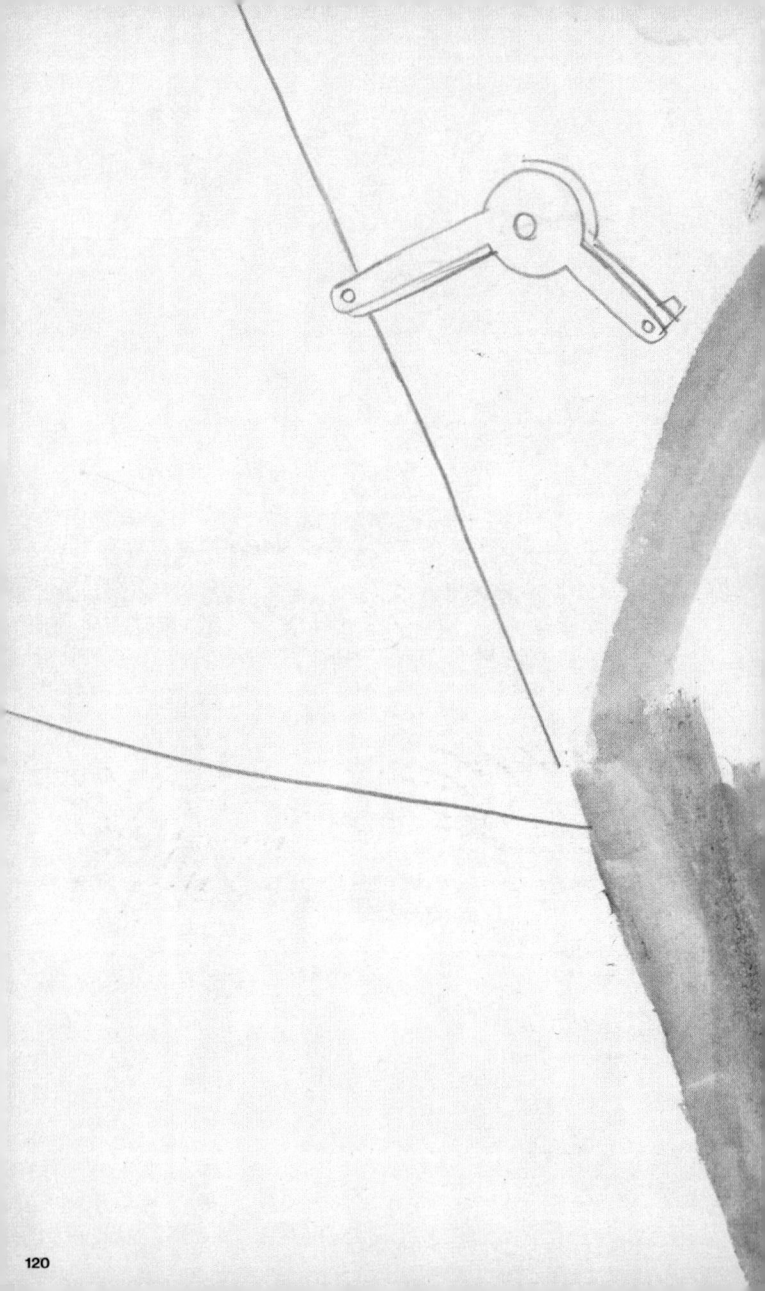

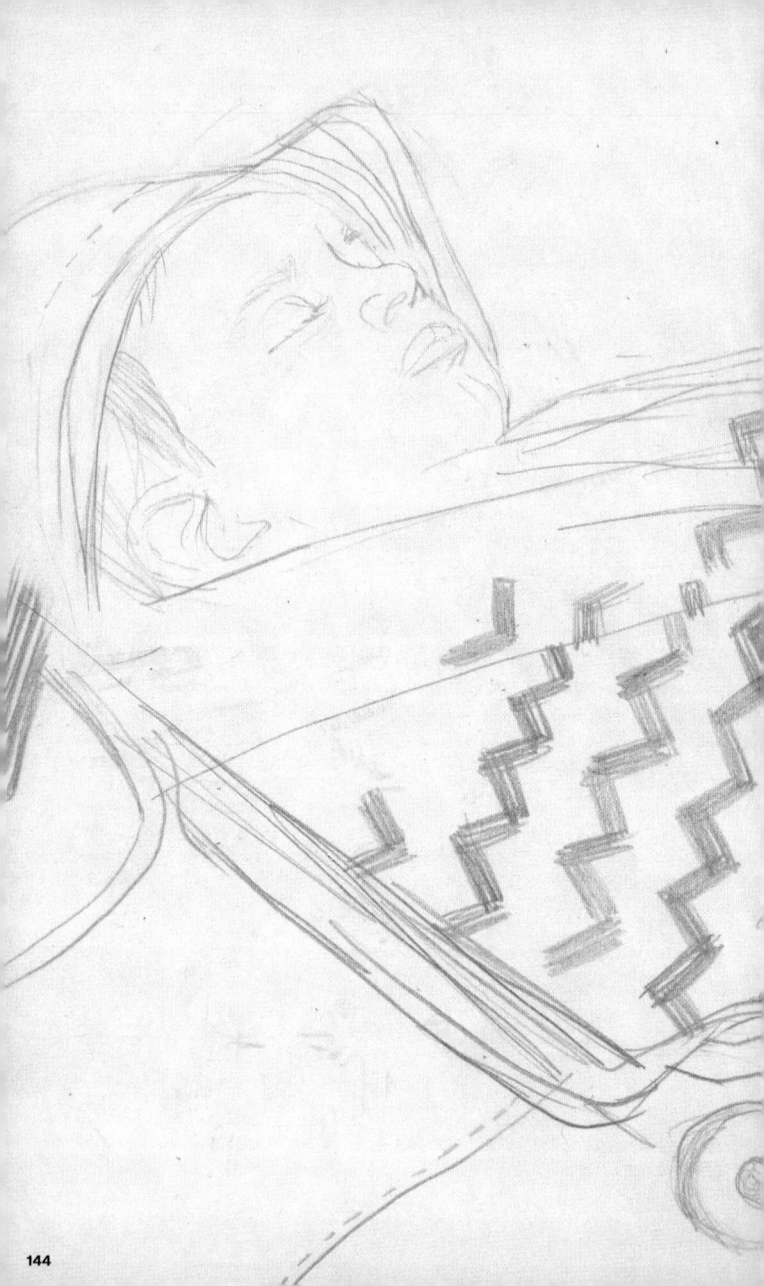

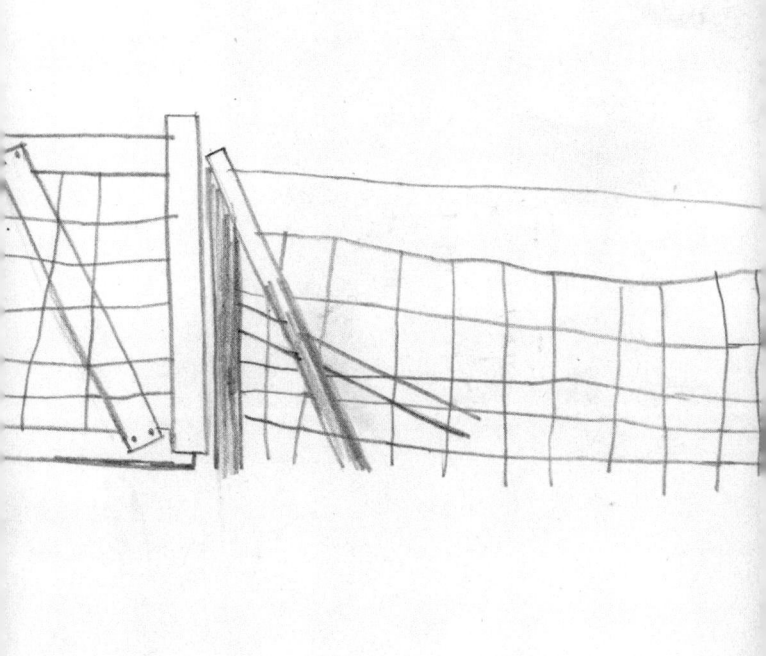

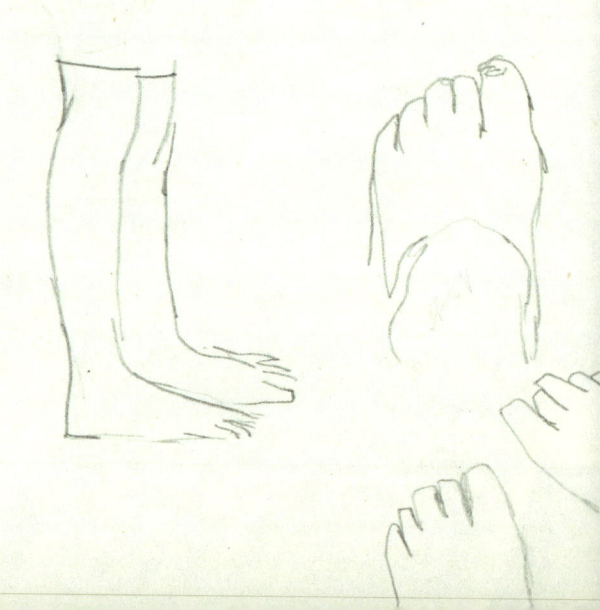

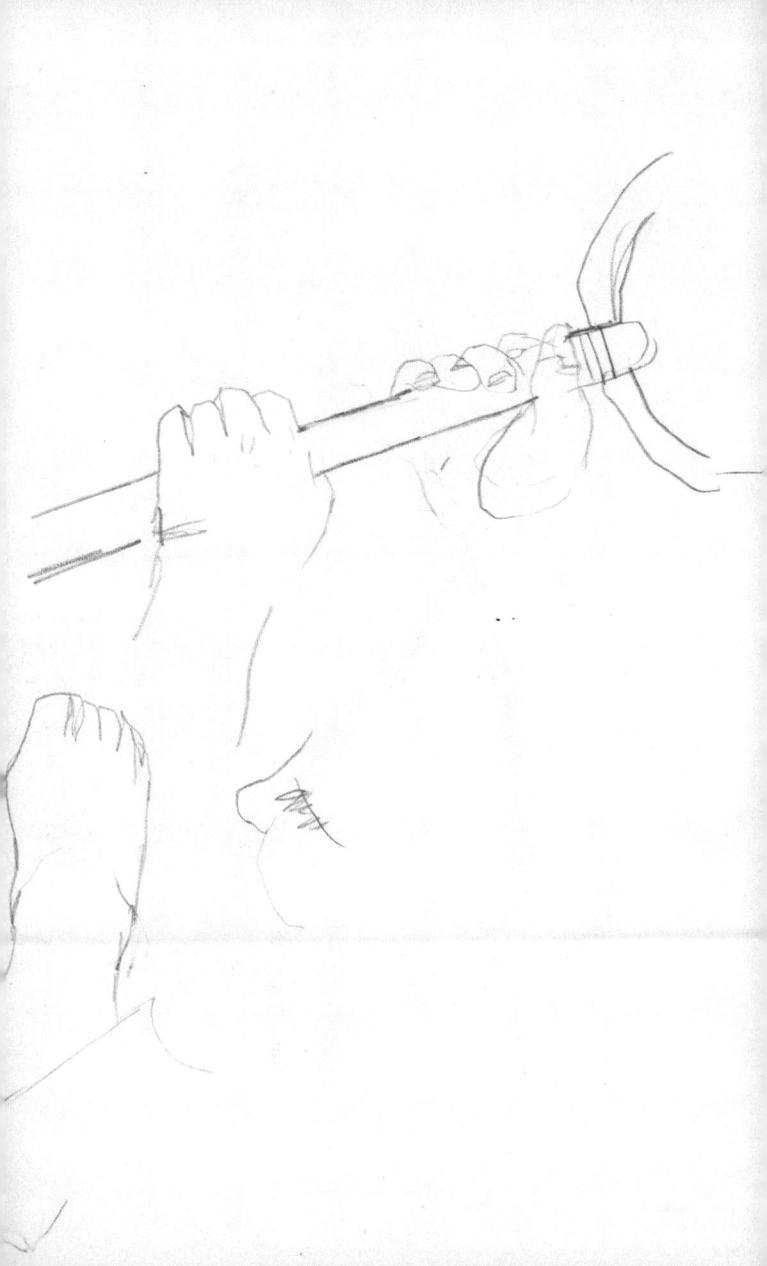

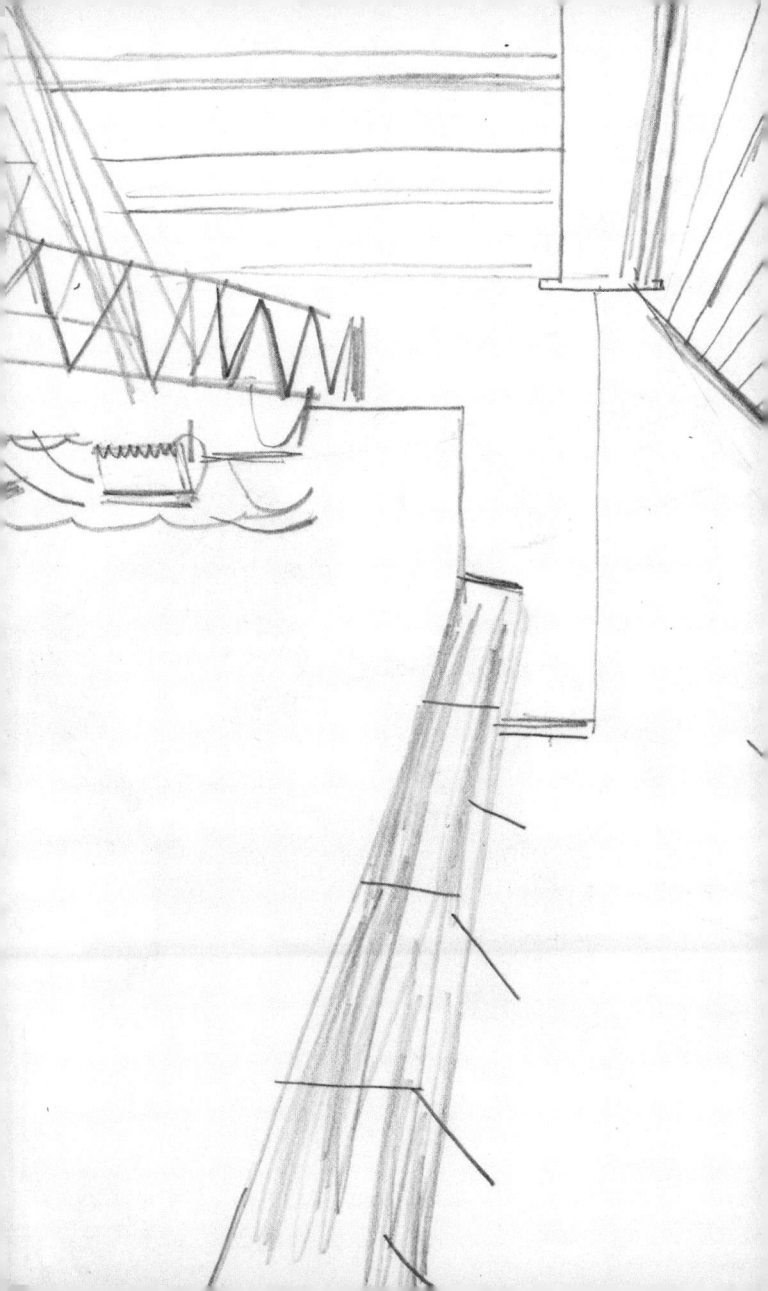

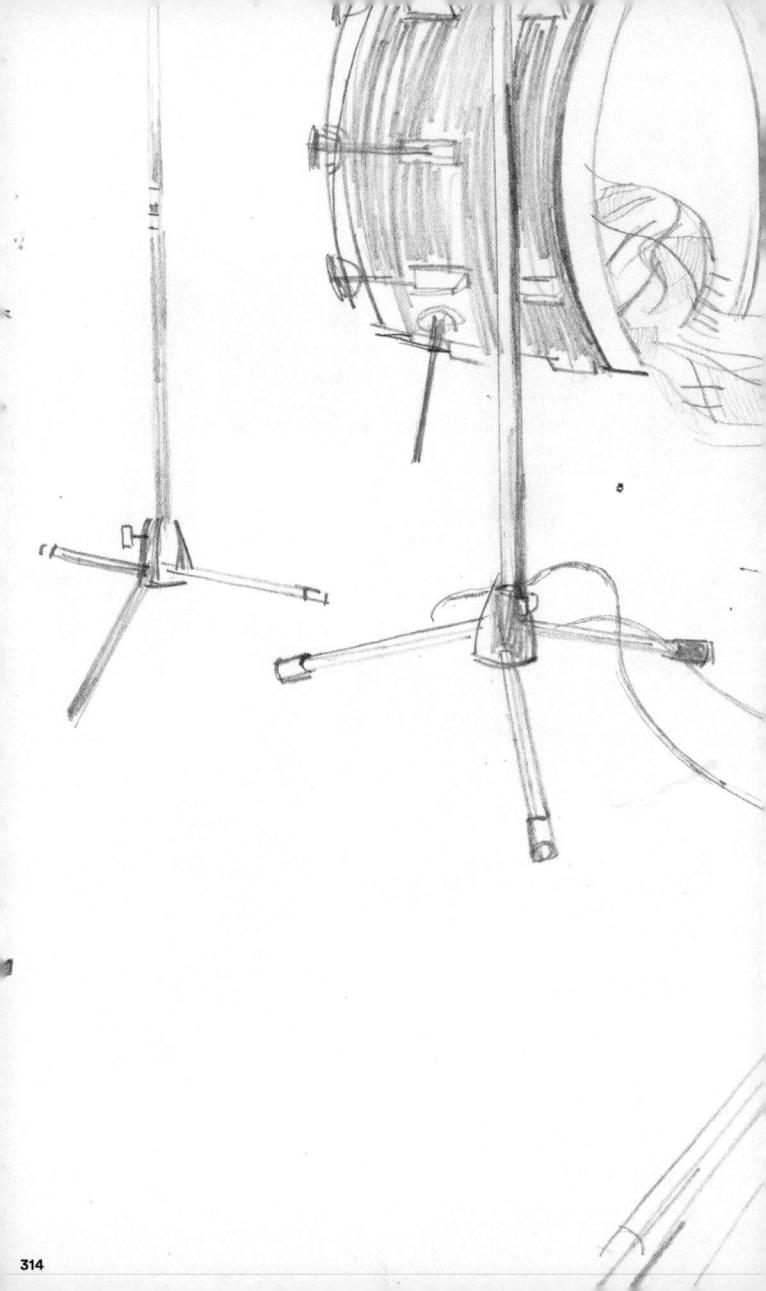

	212.		265.
	213.		266. Emerald - Australia
	214.		267.
	215.		268. St Kilda - Australia
	216.		269.
	217.		270. Geelong - Australia
	218.		271.
Stellenbosch - South Africa	219.		272. Melbourne - Australia
	220.		273.
	221.		274.
	222.		275.
	223.		276. Zaventem - Belgium
	224.		277.
Santa Monica - USA	225.		278. Angoulême - France
	226.		279.
Oceanside - USA	227.		280.
	228.		281.
	229.		282. Amsterdam - The Netherlands
	230. New York - USA		283.
Malmö - Sweden	231.		284. Bangkok - Thailand
	232.		285.
	233.		286.
	234.		287.
	235.		288.
	236.		289.
Leuven - Belgium	237.		290.
	238. Cerfontaine - Belgium		291.
2016	239.		292.
Angoulême - France	240. Berlin - Germany		293.
	241.		294.
	242.		295.
	243.		296. Destelheide - Belgium
	244. Portland - USA		297.
Antwerp - Belgium	245.		298. Geneva - Switzerland
	246.		299.
Bangkok - Thailand	247.		300.
	248.		301.
	249.		302.
	250.		303.
Koh Jum - Thailand	251.		304. Sauen - Germany
	252. Snoqualmie - USA		305.
Rome - Italy	253.		306.
			307.
	2017		308.
	254. Emerald - Australia		309.
London - United Kingdom	255.		310.
	256. Beaconsfield Upper - Australia		311.
	257.		312. Berlin - Germany
	258. Belgrave - Australia		313.
Bordeaux - France	259.		314. Merksem - Belgium
	260. Newlands Arm - Australia		315.
Chicago - USA	261.		316.
	262.		317.
	263.		
	264. Raymond Island - Australia		

re/collection
impressions from the road

by Ephameron

D/2017/9174/9
ISBN 9789 492 672 025
NUR 360, 640

All artworks in this book were made between 2011-2017 by Ephameron / Eva Cardon
www.ephameron.com

Layout: Gerard Leysen

All rights reserved
First Printing: December 2017

© 2017 Ephameron and Oogachtend, Leuven
www.oogachtend.be

No part of this publication may be reproduced and/or transmitted in any form or by any means without written permission from the publisher.